LEARN JAPANESE
FOR KIDS

Japanese Language Book For Developing A Bilingual Child

Published By

TINY TALKS
PUBLISHING

LISTEN & LEARN

Scan the QR code to hear every word pronounced
in Japanese by a native speaker.

Practice along and master each
word's sound with ease.

**Just watch, listen, and repeat—
perfect for little learners and parents
too!**

TINY TALKS
PUBLISHING

GESTURES | 挨拶 AISATSU

Hello
KONNICHIWA
こんにちは

Goodbye
SAYŌNARA
さようなら

Good Morning
OHAYŌ GOZAIMASU
おはようございます

Good Night
OYASUMINASAI
おやすみなさい

Thank You
ARIGATŌ
ありがとう

Sorry
GOMEN NASAI
ごめんなさい

Welcome
YŌKOSO
ようこそ

FAMILY | 家族 KAZOKU

Father
OTŌSAN
お父さん

Mother
OKĀSAN
お母さん

Grandfather
OJĪSAN
おじいさん

Grandmother
OBĀSAN
おばあさん

Older Brother
ONĪSAN
おにいさん

Older Sister
ONĒSAN
おねえさん

Baby
AKACHAN
赤ちゃん

COLORS | 色 IRO

Purple
MURASAKI
紫

Brown
CHAIRO
茶色

Black
KURO
黒

White
SHIRO
白

Gold
KIN'IRO
金色

Silver
GIN'IRO
銀色

SHAPES | 形 KATACHI

Circle
MARU
まる

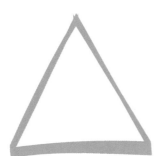

Triangle
SANKAKU
三角

Square
SHIKAKU
しかく

Oval
DAEN
楕円

Rectangle
NAGASHIKAKU
ながしかく

Diamond
HISHIGATA
ひしがた

Heart
HĀTO-GATA
ハート形

FEELINGS | きもち KIMOCHI

Happy
SHIAWASE
幸せ

Sad
KANASHII
悲しい

Angry
OKORU
怒る

Excited
YOROKOBU
喜ぶ

Proud
**HOKORINI
OMOU**
誇りに思う

Tired
TSUKARETA
疲れた

Bored
TSUMARANAI
つまらない

Worried
SHINPAI SURU
心配する

Scared
KOWAGARU
怖がる

ROUTINE | 日課 NIKKA

Wake Up
OKIRU
起きる

Brush Teeth
HA O MIGAKU
歯を磨く

Wash Face
KAO O ARAU
顔を洗う

Bathe
OFURO NI HAIRU
お風呂に入る

Get Dressed
FUKU O KIRU
服を着る

Eat Breakfast
ASAGOHAN O TABERU
朝ごはんを食べる

ROUTINE | 日課 NIKKA

Go To School
GAKKŌ NI IKU
学校に行く

Go To Bed
NERU
寝る

Study
BENKYŌ SURU
勉強する

Eat Dinner
YORUGOHAN O TABERU
夜ごはんを食べる

FOOD | 食べ物 TABEMONO

Bread
PAN
パン

Milk
GYŪNYŪ
牛乳

Egg
TAMAGO
卵

Cheese
CHĪZU
チーズ

Rice
GOHAN
ご飯

Water
MIZU
水

Juice
JŪSU
ジュース

Cereal
SHIRIARU
シリアル

FOOD | 食べ物 TABEMONO

Cake
KĒKI
ケーキ

Cookie
KUKKĪ
クッキー

Candy
KYANDI
キャンディ

Meat
NIKU
肉

Fish
SAKANA
魚

Jelly
ZERĪ
ゼリー

Soup
SŪPU
スープ

Pasta
PASUTA
パスタ

FOOD | 食べ物 TABEMONO

Ice Cream
AISUKURĪMU
アイスクリーム

Salt
SHIO
塩

Sugar
SATŌ
砂糖

Salad
SARADA
サラダ

Chocolate
CHOKORĒTO
チョコレート

Coffee
KŌHĪ
コーヒー

Tea
OCHA
お茶

VEGETABLES | 野菜 YASAI

Tomato
TOMATO
トマト

Potato
JAGAIMO
じゃがいも

Peas
MAME
豆

Corn
TŌMOROKOSHI
とうもろこし

Carrot
NINJIN
にんじん

Onion
TAMANEGI
たまねぎ

FRUIT | 果物 KUDAMONO

Apple
RINGO
りんご

Banana
BANANA
バナナ

Grape
BUDŌ
ぶどう

Lemon
REMON
レモン

Orange
ORENJI
オレンジ

Pineapple
PAINAPPURU
パイナップル

Strawberry
ICHIGO
いちご

Watermelon
SUIKA
スイカ

FACE | 顔 KAO

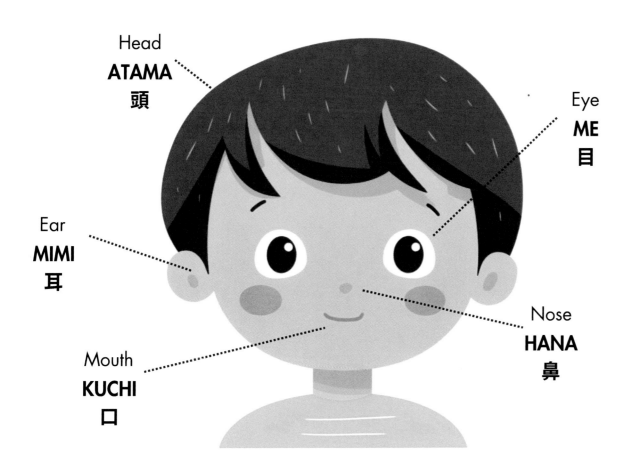

Head
ATAMA
頭

Eye
ME
目

Ear
MIMI
耳

Nose
HANA
鼻

Mouth
KUCHI
口

DESCRIPTIONS | 説明
SETSUMEI

Big
ŌKII
大きい

Small
CHISAI
小さい

Cold
SAMUI
寒い

Hot
ATSUI
熱い

Long
NAGAI
長い

Short
MIJIKAI
短い

Wet
NURETA
濡れた

Dry
KAWAITA
乾いた

DESCRIPTIONS | 説明
SETSUMEI

Empty
KARA
空

Full
IPPAI
いっぱい

Fast
HAYAI
速い

Light
KARUI
軽い

Heavy
OMOI
重い

Old
FURUI
古い

New
ATARASHII
新しい

Soft
YAWARAKAI
柔らかい

Hard
KATAI
硬い

Slow
OSOI
遅い

NUMBERS | 数字 SŪJI

1 2 3 4 5

One	Two	Three	Four	Five
ICHI	**NI**	**SAN**	**SHI/YON**	**GO**
一	二	三	四	五

6 7 8 9 10

Six	Seven	Eight	Nine	Ten
ROKU	**SHICHI/NANA**	**HACHI**	**KYŪ/KU**	**JŪ**
六	七	八	九	十

NUMBERS | 数字 SŪJI

20

Twenty
NI-JŪ
二十

30

Thirty
SAN-JŪ
三十

40

Forty
SHI-JŪ/YON-JŪ
四十

50

Fifty
GO-JŪ
五十

60

Sixty
ROKU-JŪ
六十

70

Seventy
SHICHI-JŪ/NANA-JŪ
七十

Eighty
HACHI-JŪ
八十

Ninety
KYŪ-JŪ/KU-JŪ
九十

One Hundred
HYAKU
百

TOYS | おもちゃ OMOCHA

Toy
OMOCHA
おもちゃ

Ball
BŌRU
ボール

Doll
NINGYŌ
人形

Teddy
TEDIBEA
テディーベア

Book
HON
本

Crayon
KUREYON
クレヨン

TOYS | おもちゃ OMOCHA

Drum
DORAMU
ドラム

Guitar
GITĀ
ギター

Slide
SUBERIDAI
滑り台

Sand
SUNA
砂

Bucket
BAKETSU
バケツ

Shovel
SHABERU
シャベル

ACTIONS | 動作 DŌSA

Eat
TABERU
食べる

Drink
NOMU
飲む

Play
ASOBU
遊ぶ

Run
HASHIRU
走る

Walk
ARUKU
歩く

Sit
SUWARU
座る

Stand
TATSU
立つ

Jump
TOBU
跳ぶ

ACTIONS | 動作 DŌSA

Dance
ODORU
踊る

Sing
UTAU
歌う

Laugh
WARAU
笑う

Cry
NAKU
泣く

Write
KAKU
書く

Read
YOMU
読む

Watch
MIRU
見る

Listen
KIKU
聞く

ACTIONS | 動作 DŌSA

Open
AKERU
開ける

Close
SHIMERU
閉める

Climb
NOBORU
登る

Swing
YURERU
揺れる

Catch
TSUKAMAERU
捕まえる

Throw
NAGERU
投げる

Wash
ARAU
洗う

ACTIONS | 動作 DŌSA

Think
KANGAERU
考える

Kiss
KISU SURU
キスする

Draw
KAKU
描く

Hug
DAKISHIMERU
抱きしめる

ANIMALS | 動物 DŌBUTSU

Dog
INU
犬

Cat
NEKO
猫

Fish
SAKANA
魚

Bird
TORI
鳥

Horse
UMA
馬

Cow
USHI
牛

Chicken
NIWATORI
鶏

Duck
AHIRU
あひる

ANIMALS | 動物 DŌBUTSU

Sheep
HITSUJI
羊

Pig
BUTA
豚

Rabbit
USAGI
兎

Bear
KUMA
熊

Elephant
ZŌ
象

Lion
RAION
ライオン

Tiger
TORA
虎

Monkey
SARU
猿

ANIMALS | 動物 DŌBUTSU

Giraffe
KIRIN
キリン

Bee
HACHI
蜂

Mouse
NEZUMI
ネズミ

Frog
KAERU
蛙

Snake
HEBI
蛇

Turtle
KAME
亀

Penguin
PENGUIN
ペンギン

Zebra
SHIMAUMA
シマウマ

ANIMALS | 動物 DŌBUTSU

Whale
KUJIRA
鯨

Dolphin
IRUKA
イルカ

Butterfly
CHŌCHŌ
ちょうちょ

Spider
KUMO
蜘蛛

Owl
FUKURŌ
梟

BODY | 体 KARADA

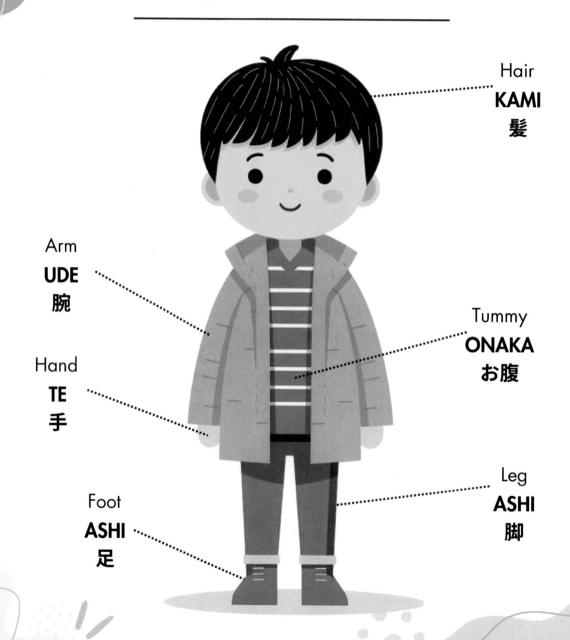

Hair
KAMI
髪

Arm
UDE
腕

Hand
TE
手

Tummy
ONAKA
お腹

Foot
ASHI
足

Leg
ASHI
脚

DIRECTIONS | 方向 HŌKŌ

Far
TŌI
遠い

Up
UE
上

Right
MIGI
右

Near
CHIKAI
近い

Left
HIDARI
左

Inside
UCHIGAWA
内側

Down
SHITA
下

Outside
SOTOGAWA
外側

HOME | 家 IE

House
IE
家

Door
DOA
ドア

Window
MADO
窓

Bed
BEDDO
ベッド

Chair
ISU
椅子

Room
HEYA
部屋

Bathroom
OFUROBA
お風呂場

Television
TEREBI
テレビ

HOME | 家 IE

Sofa
SOFA
ソファ

Clock
TOKEI
時計

Pillow
MAKURA
枕

Blanket
MŌFU
毛布

Bookshelf
HONDANA
本棚

Mirror
KAGAMI
鏡

Bath
OFURO
お風呂

Sink
SHINKU
シンク

HOME | 家 IE

Desk

TSUKUE

机

Lamp

RANPU

ランプ

Drawer

HIKIDASHI

引き出し

SEASONS | 季節 KISETSU

Spring
HARU
春

Summer
NATSU
夏

Fall
AKI
秋

Winter
FUYU
冬

KITCHEN | 台所 DAIDOKORO

Table
TĒBURU
テーブル

Kitchen
DAIDOKORO
台所

Fridge
REIZŌKO
冷蔵庫

Oven
ŌBUN
オーブン

Pot
NABE
鍋

KITCHEN | 台所 DAIDOKORO

Fork
FŌKU
フォーク

Spoon
SUPŪN
スプーン

Knife
NAIFU
ナイフ

Bowl
BŌRU
ボウル

Cup
KAPPU
カップ

CLOTHES | 洋服 YŌFUKU

Shirt
SHATSU
シャツ

Pants
PANTSU
パンツ

Dress
DORESU
ドレス

Hat
BŌSHI
帽子

Socks
KUTSUSHITA
靴下

Shoes
KUTSU
靴

Coat
KŌTO
コート

Gloves
TEBUKURO
手袋

CLOTHES | 洋服 YŌFUKU

Scarf
SUKĀFU
スカーフ

Pajamas
PAJAMA
パジャマ

Skirt
SUKĀTO
スカート

Boots
BŪTSU
ブーツ

Slippers
SURIPPA
スリッパ

T-Shirt
T-SHATSU
Tシャツ

Shorts
SHŌTO PANTSU
ショートパンツ

Sweater
SĒTĀ
セーター

NATURE | 自然 SHIZEN

Star
HOSHI
星

Sky
SORA
空

Rain
AME
雨

Snow
YUKI
雪

Tree
KI
木

Flower
HANA
花

Leaf
HAPPA
葉っぱ

Grass
KUSA
草

NATURE | 自然 SHIZEN

Cloud
KUMO
雲

River
KAWA
川

Lake
MIZŪMI
湖

Ocean
UMI
海

Stone
ISHI
石

Beach
KAI-GAN
海岸

Mountain
YAMA
山

Wind
KAZE
風

Plant
SHOKUBUTSU
植物

PLACES | 場所 BASHO

Farm
NŌJŌ
農場

Garden
NIWA
庭

Playground
ASOBIBA
遊び場

Airport
KŪKŌ
空港

School
GAKKŌ
学校

PLACES | 場所 BASHO

Park
KŌEN
公園

Road
DŌRO
道路

Bridge
HASHI
橋

Store
MISE
店

VEHICLES I
乗り物 NORIMONO

Bus
BASU
バス

Car
KURUMA
車

Truck
TORAKKU
トラック

Boat
BŌTO
ボート

Plane
HIKŌKI
飛行機

Train
DENSHA
電車

VEHICLES I
乗り物 NORIMONO

Bicycle
JITENSHA
自転車

Ship
FUNE
船

Taxi
TAKUSHĪ
タクシー

Motorcycle
ŌTOBAI
オートバイ

Helicopter
HERIKOPUTĀ
ヘリコプター

Balloon
KIKYŪ
気球

PROFESSIONS I
職業 SHOKUGYŌ

Chef
SHEFU
シェフ

Police
KEISATSUKAN
警察官

Firefigher
SHŌBŌSHI
消防士

Farmer
NŌKA
農家

Artist
GEIJUTSUKA
芸術家

Dentist
SHIKA-I
歯科医

PROFESSIONS I
職業 SHOKUGYŌ

Doctor
ISHA
医者

Teacher
SENSEI
先生

Engineer
ENJINIA
エンジニア

Lawyer
BENGOSHI
弁護士

Nurse
KANGOSHI
看護師

TIME | 時間 JIKAN

Day
HIRU
昼

Night
YORU
夜

Morning
ASA
朝

Afternoon
GOGO
午後

Evening
YŪGATA
夕方

Made in the USA
Las Vegas, NV
18 December 2024

14536993R00031